Lance's last major project, a collaboration with another local photographer, Charles Peterson, was *Place/Date,* a Pearl Jam retrospective book of photos. For the last five years Lance has been performing in a band of his own called The Briefs. After many tours and three full-length records his focus has again returned to the darkroom.

Music was my first love, but it was never just an audio track. I experienced it in terms of the community it came out of. When I discovered The Clash, there was no looking back. I was clearly in their camp before they ever existed, thanks to the parallel world my pirate-radio-DJ dad introduced me to. Later, the Seattle punk scene was so small it felt like a family whose little get-togethers got out of hand. I was fascinated by the life of rock and the cathartic ritual between fan and musician. I borrowed my dad's camera and started seizing the moments, documenting the shows. I loved the energy—loud and fast. Through the punk scene I discovered a growing grassroots art scene, where I decided to spend a couple years formally studying photography.

Mostly, though, I learned from photographing my friends in bands who needed photos. They had ideas of fame, whatever that was, and I had a hunger to feed it. Some of them were great, even if it was only for the duration of a two-minute tune, three-minute video, or six-gig van tour. Others became Soundgarden, Nirvana, and Pearl Jam, to name a few. I had no idea where all this was going; I was there for the ride. For five years I focused on photographing Pearl Jam, shooting as close to the action as possible. I thought crisscrossing the world with Pearl Jam would be about late-night parties and TVs soaring out of hotel windows. Instead, it was long periods of stillness punctuated by intense outbursts of energy.

Pearl Jam was a moving target. I learned to adjust to the surroundings and never went anywhere without my camera. On the first stop of my first tour with them, in San Francisco, I was stunned by how tall the stage was compared to the sweaty, 199-seat clubs we were used to. The audience had exploded overnight. To capture that show, I relied on the words of Robert Capa: "If your pictures aren't good enough, you aren't close enough"; quickly made friends with all the security guards; and crawled around on stage to get the best possible angles as the band jumped around with reckless abandon. From that show I learned to always carry longer lenses.

I used to sit and obsessively study the photographs on my record jackets while listening to the albums repeatedly. I had my own story for why Keith Richards was leaning perilously in a hotel hallway, or Sid Vicious had blood running down his chest on stage, or The Ramones looked so pissed off on a New York street corner. I never thought during my years of trying to emulate my photographic heroes that my prints would someday end up in a book. But here they are, and somebody is destined to sit listening to Pearl Jam and studying these pictures. All I can say is: look out. You never know where the pictures and music will take you.

—Lance Mercer

Lance Mercer

These wonderful photographs show something we knew all along: being in a band is cool, glamorous (in a scruffy beat-poet, garage-attendant way), continual, and colorful. In the case of Pearl Jam, the musician's life also manages to look serious and happy at the same time. Great photographs like these are in themselves musical, so they add an extra track.

—Pete Townshend

Pete Townshend

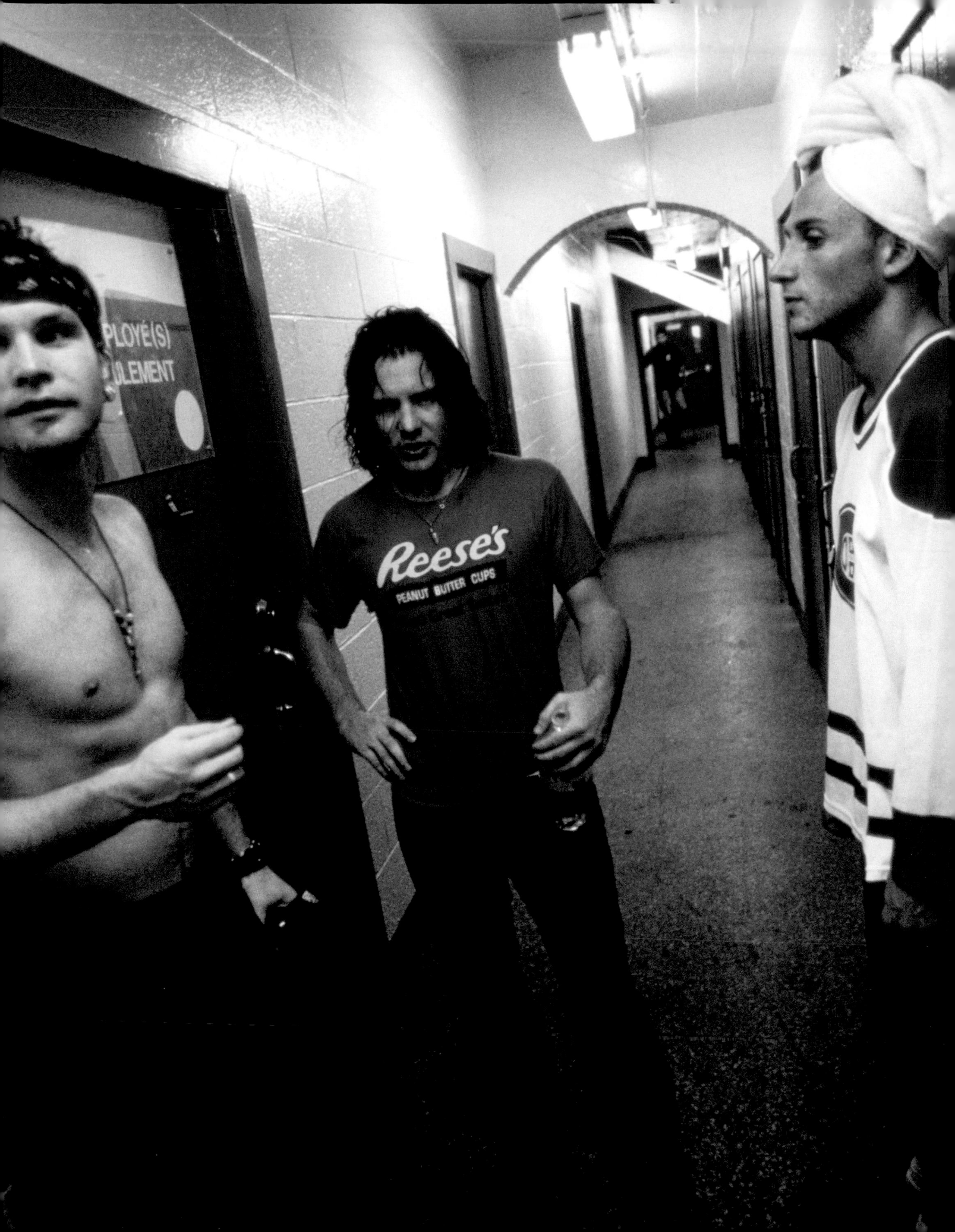
PLOYÉ(S)
ULEMENT
Reese's
PEANUT BUTTER CUPS

I first met Lance Mercer in the early '80s. He was known to us as "the Nice Bopo." The Bopo Boys were an unruly gang of West Coast skate punks who wore crudely decorated, sleeveless jean jackets over leather motorcycle jackets. They created disturbances whenever and wherever possible. In a pinch one could talk reason with Lance, who would then sometimes act as mediator when the Bopos would, say, invade your party uninvited, with not the best intentions in mind. Lance stood out with his shock of curly red hair, easygoing demeanor, and curiosity about things besides getting fucked up. It was obvious he wasn't in for the long-haul life of a juvenile delinquent, and would soon move past hooliganism for bigger and better things. In my book there is a photo of Lance in all his Bopo glory, forty-ouncer in hand, bursting to the front of a small crowd in some dingy basement about to watch some grungy band. I didn't actually discover that photo in my archives until seventeen years after I took it. It was terribly washed-out on the original proof sheet and I couldn't tell who was actually in the photo, but as the image appeared on my computer screen postscanning, there was Lance! The Nice Bopo.

Photography turned out to be Lance's calling. He set aside the Bopo colors and started appearing at shows with a 35mm SLR and flash in hand. We soon divided up camps: I went the Mudhoney/Nirvana/Sub Pop route; Lance, the Mother Love Bone/Alice/Temple/Pearl Jam road. Certainly our paths would cross both socially and professionally on many occasions. He would often turn to me for advice, both practical and delicate, which I was always happy to give. We would do the book *Place/Date* together, and just recently Lance had me talk to a class he's been teaching on rock-and-roll photography.

Lance has never lost that punk rock charisma (once a punk, always a punk, I say). He took a hiatus from photography to flirt with the other side, playing bass in the retro-punk outfit The Briefs, a band as great as those Lance is known for photographing. Now he's juggling both rock stardom (wink) and photography, as well as continuing to be a loving and dedicated father to his daughters (and throwing them the occasional new wave disco birthday party). Some of Lance's best pictures are of his daughters. I know that Lance is in love with photography most when he's doing it for himself, whether it be of a band he loves or his family. That organic quality is his strongest suit. Nothing fancy—just good old-fashioned photography.

Lance's name will always be synonomous with the image of Pearl Jam. It's a long, dedicated body of work, and deserves to be seen in a book such as this. The photographs here also show the band's dedication to Lance, and rightly so. In 1996 I went on tour in Europe for a couple of weeks with Pearl Jam. As I was the only photographer allowed for the whole show, inevitably, fans would come up afterward to find out who I was. Are you Lance Mercer? they would excitedly ask. No, would come my reply, Charles Peterson. Nine times out of ten I'd draw a blank, and the fan would turn away, disappointed they weren't able to finally meet Lance in the flesh, the closest they'd probably ever get to Pearl Jam themselves. They had experienced the lives of their heroes through Lance's camera, living vicariously through his access and talent at capturing the band's music and personality. Those disappointed fans spoke volumes. I'm sure Lance would agree with me—this book is for them.

—Charles Peterson

Charles Peterson

first song, first show. "release." moore theatre. seattle.
even then, pearl jam was something a little more personal, a little
more passionate than you were prepared for, already with a history
steeped in pain and rebirth and a deep-running love of music. it felt
like a club, in the best way. still does. every album, every show still
resonates like a bootleg, smuggled directly from the band to you.
and every one of lance's great photos pulses with that spirit. this is
the backstage, onstage, every stage journey of pearl jam, forever
strapped to the muse. so pick your disc, or spin your vinyl, and
turn it way up. these images are meant to be listened to, loud.

—cameron crowe

cameron crowe

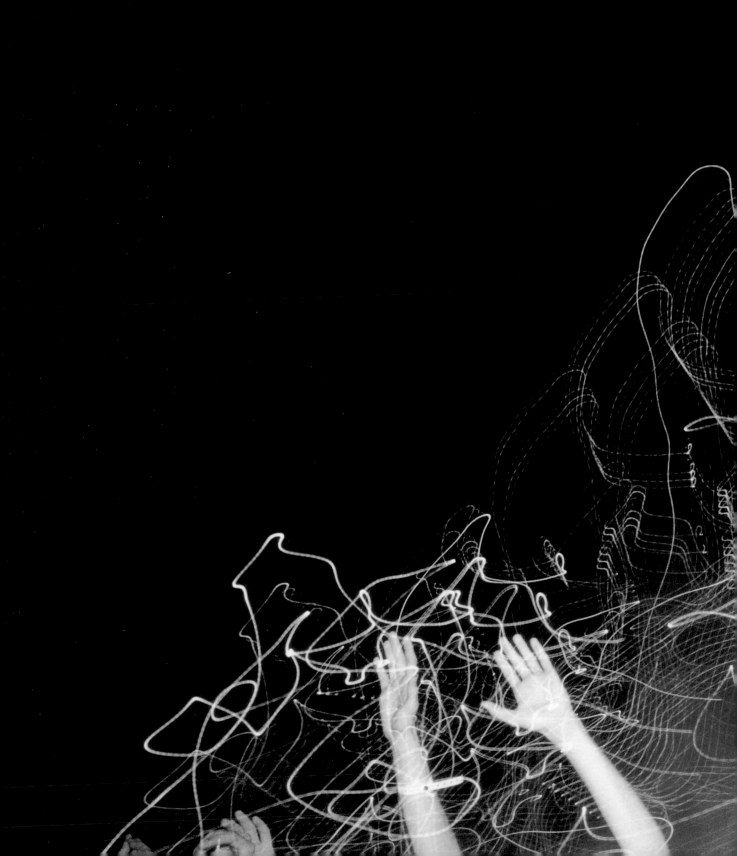

Anyone who was ever touched by Pearl Jam's
music will treasure this document of the band's early years. I feel
so fortunate to have been there during this period as a witness,
participant, sister, and (mostly!) a fan, experiencing their journey
from the start, watching the evolution of Mother Love Bone into
one of those rare rock bands that not only achieves success, but
does so on their own terms and forever remains relevant. Remem-
bering everything so vividly, feeling that part of my life entwined with
their story, their music, their struggles and their triumphs—these
candid, intimate photos capture the band, and that inspiring period,
so perfectly.

—Michele Anthony

Michele Anthony

I was checkin' out the competition in the early '90s and came back from the record store with the latest crop of young bands. I'd heard "Alive" on the radio and so I settled into my car in front of my house (my favorite listening spot) and popped in *Ten*.

The first thing I noticed was the warmth of their sound even though the band was hitting hard. They had the ability to play hard and swing at the same time. The music felt composed and powerful with a lot of complementary interplay among the instruments. These are the qualities that suggest the presence of a real band. Listen to The Who and Led Zeppelin . . . rockin' and swingin'. Also the personalness of the songs and sound. They felt like a band intent on meaning something to its audience . . . to you. They were not pop formalists. There was a lot of fresh air in the songwriting and arrangements; the song structures were sometimes unconventional, heralding back to older pre-rock music.

The singer had a trill in his voice. A fast vibrato unusual for a rock singer. Also referring back to old folk songs and roots music. You felt he knew the audience he was addressing was out there. That he knew them like he knew himself . . . or was trying to. The trying was the important part. The whole effect was one of tenderness, subtlety coupled with a lot of power. They had soul. You can go a long way with that combination of elements. They did.

I got out of the car feeling like there was work to do. What more can you ask from a great rock band?

—Bruce Springsteen

Bruce Springsteen

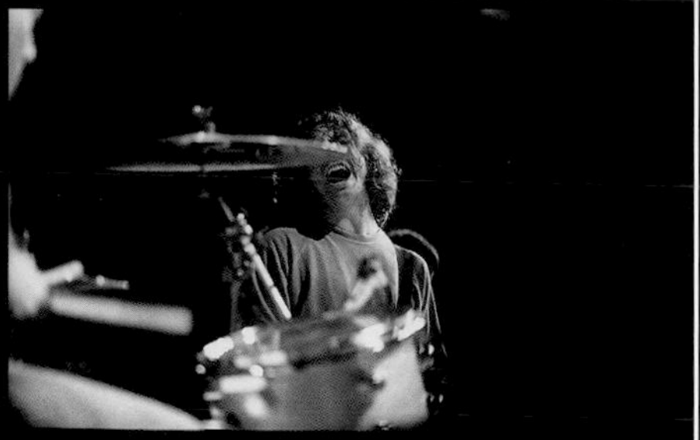
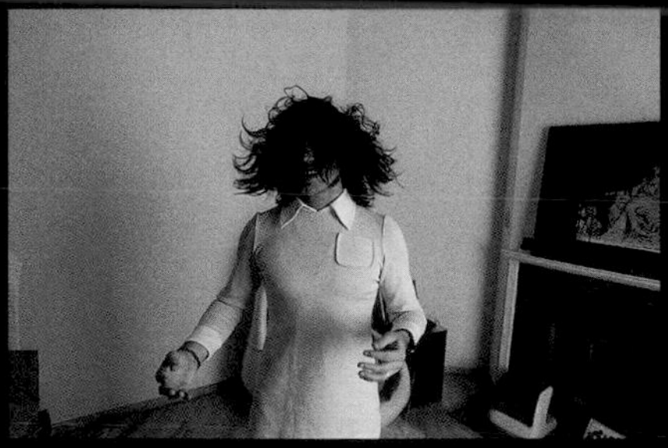
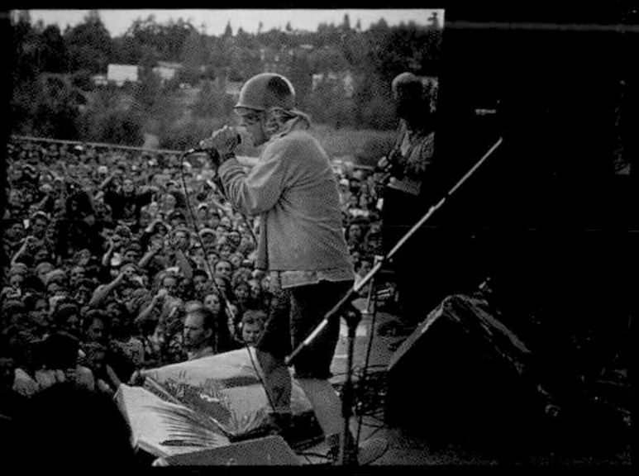
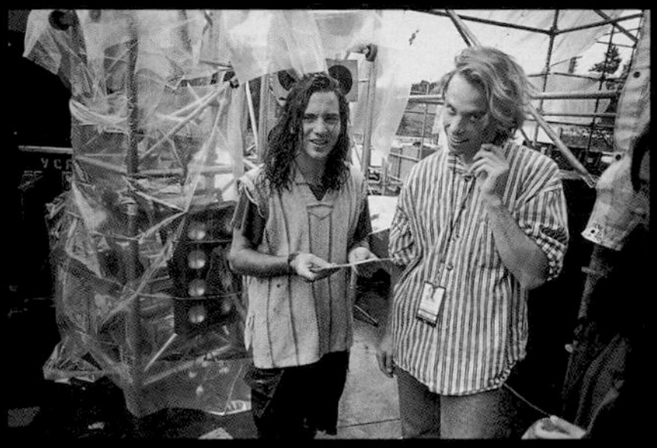
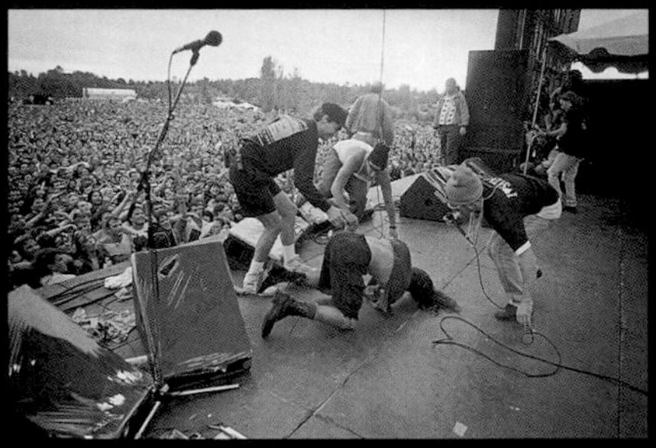
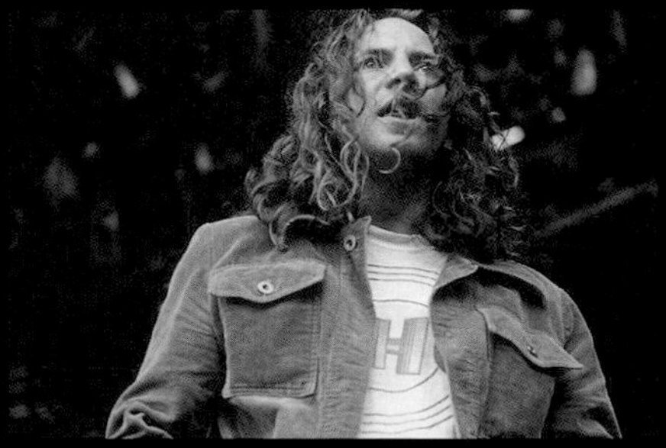
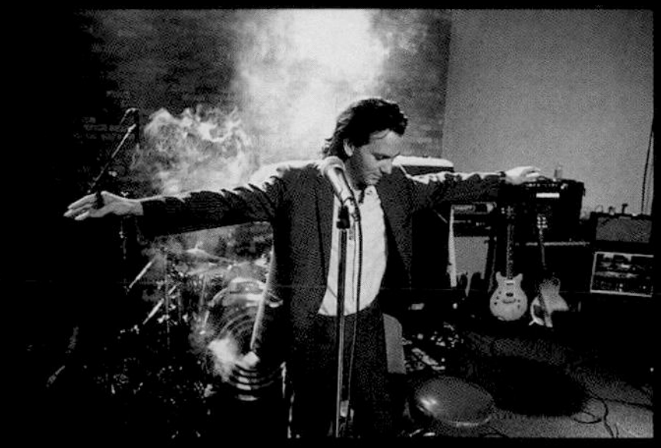
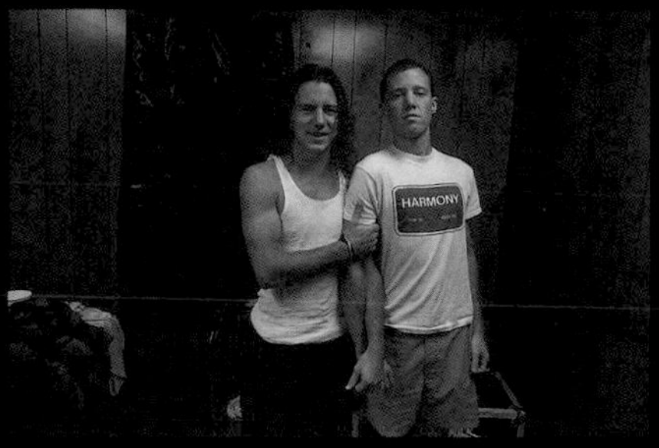
HARMONY
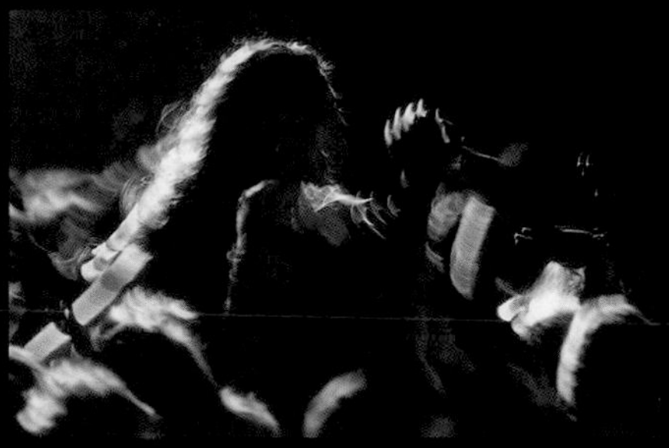
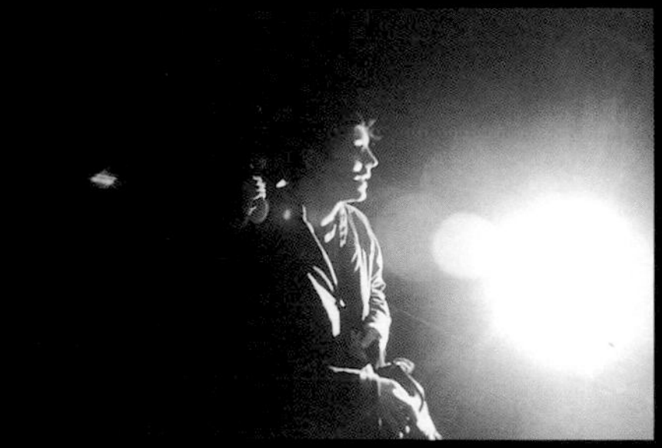
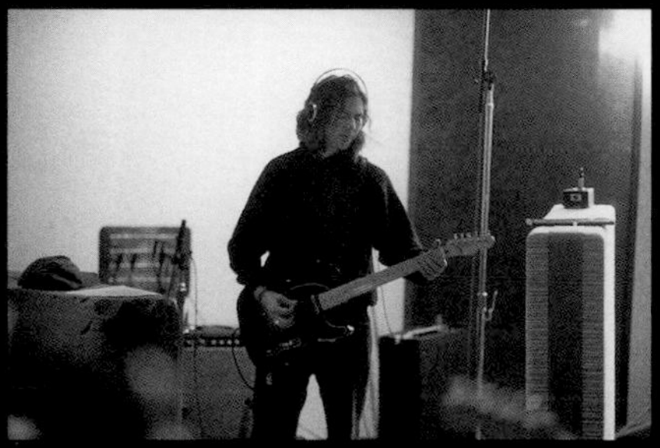
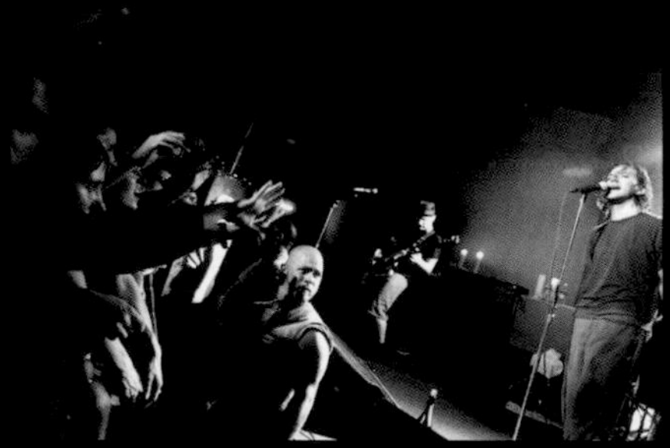
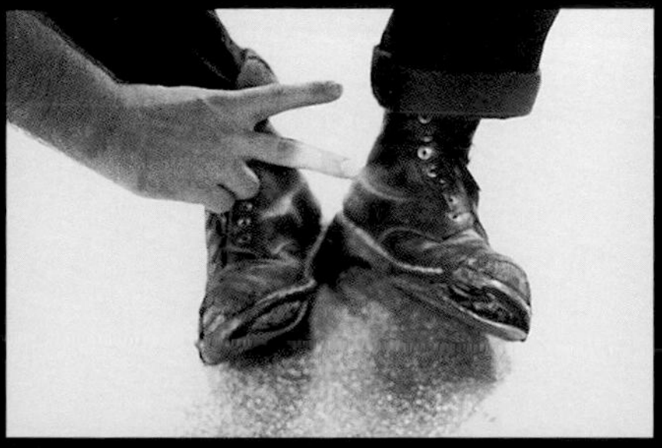
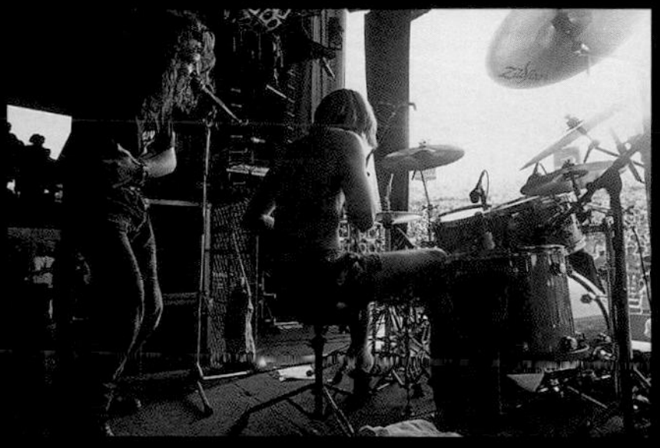
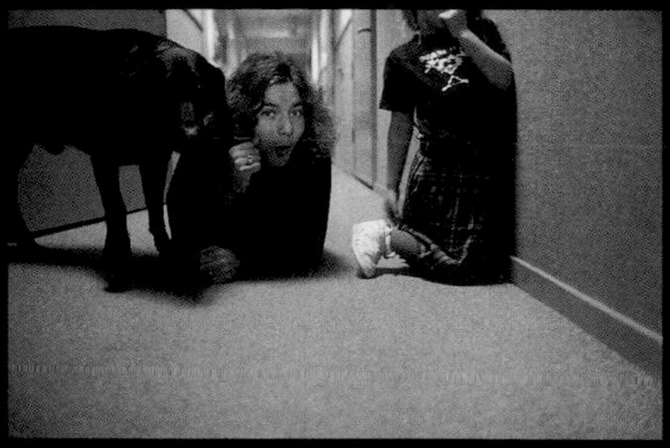

I first met Eddie Vedder when he phoned me out of the blue to say he wanted to interview me for *Interview* magazine. In subsequent meetings I found him extraordinarily modest, intelligent, widely read, and with a deep commitment to social justice.

At a recent concert in Boston, waiting to go on stage— and this tells it all about Eddie—he had a group of us listen to a lawyer who, with Eddie's help, is defending a man on death row in Arkansas.

—Howard Zinn

Howard Zinn

Things I like about Pearl Jam:

They are consistently excellent live.

They don't gouge their fans at the box office.

Great poster art and T-shirts.

We won't be hearing "Evenflow" in advertisements for cars, hair conditioner, or feminine hygiene products.

They support indie bands.

They don't do cheese.

None of them golfs regularly.

They play through injuries.

When you play their albums backwards you hear Howard Zinn reading *People's History of the United States*.

When I tried to get them to drink after-hours on tour, they cared enough about their audience the next night to go to their rooms and sleep.

No flash pots.

—Tim Robbins

Tim Robbins

When you're first off on your own and ready to take on the world, you need something to play loud, something reckless, something you can believe in and hold on to. You find it in a new band, one that knocks you on your ass. Energy, truth, and anger. The more you listen, the more personal it gets. You carry the songs in your head, and you swear you start to feel a little bit freer. It's just what you need, so you turn it all the way up, and you believe in your new favorite band.

Years later, when the working life has you slipping into the boredom of routine, you yearn to see the band play, hoping to feel firsthand the energy you've heard on their bootlegs. But nothing's routine for them now, not even a show. Loyal only to their fans and their conscience, they take on the silent enemies of the day: institutions and corporations, ignorance and apathy. Republicans. Tension is everywhere—even in the music—but the connection with the band only grows stronger. They finally get to play and you're there: it's loud, it's right, and you smile because you know you're wide awake again.

Later still, when you know it's time to find your place in life but you don't know where, you see that your favorite band has figured it out. They've been through a lot by now, more than enough to justify telling us all to fuck off. But they don't, of course, and instead carve an identity as admirable as it is unique. No principles sacrificed. No one left behind. Just enough space for the music and the fans. Their place is big enough to make a real difference but small enough to hide. You admire it from afar, put on your headphones, and go off to find your own place just the same size.

And recently, after life has placed you up on a small stage of your own, you get to meet the band you've admired for so long. You expect it to be awkward, like when you struggle to make conversation with strangers at work. But the band is genuine, warm, fun, and disarming; somehow, they make you feel like you've been around the whole time. You should have known that's the way these guys would be. The show is about to start, so you take a seat off to the side. As the lights go down and the first notes ring out, you shake your head and appreciate one more lesson from this amazing band: how to treat strangers like friends, whether onstage or off.

—Theo Epstein

Theo Epstein

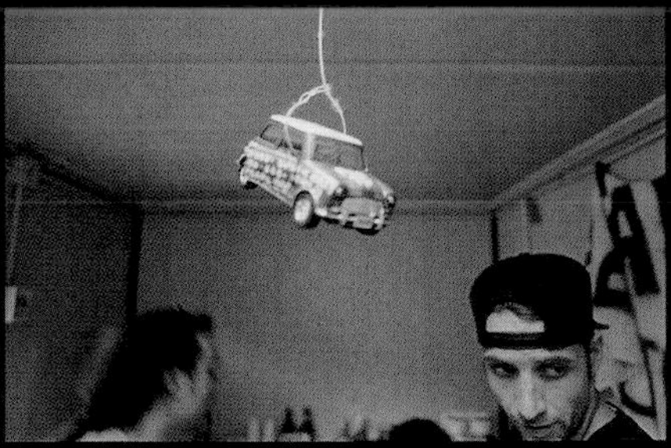
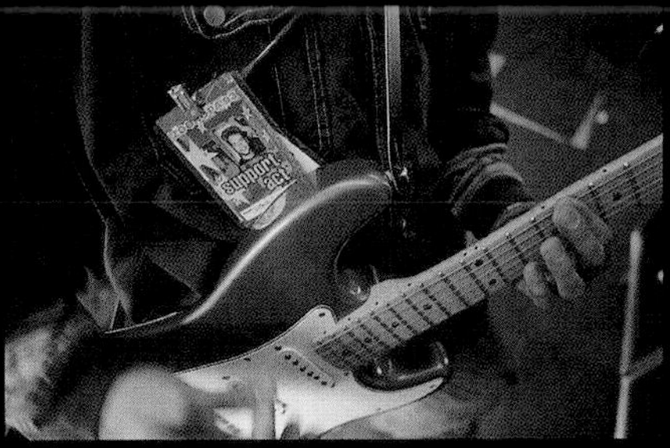
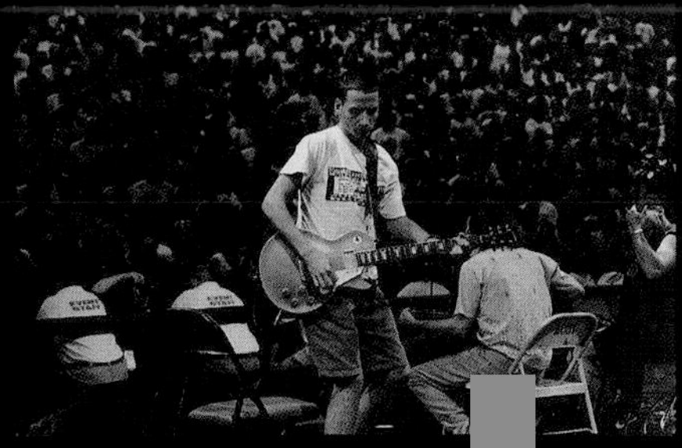
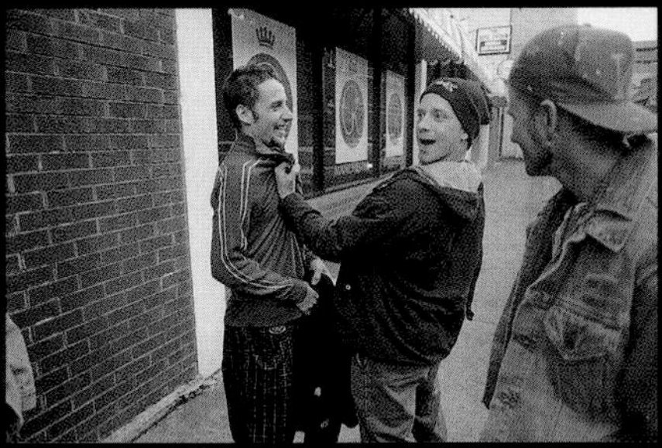
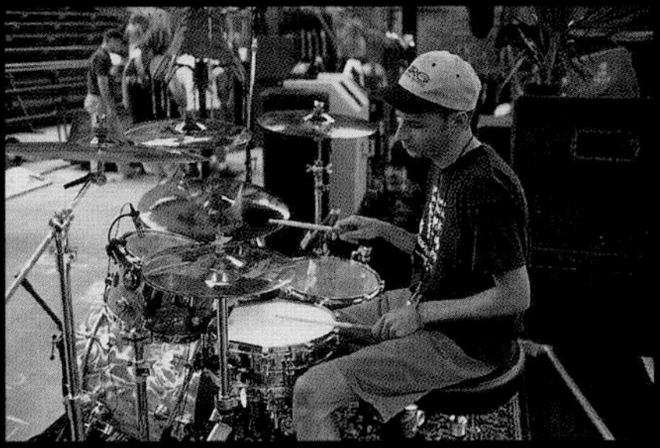
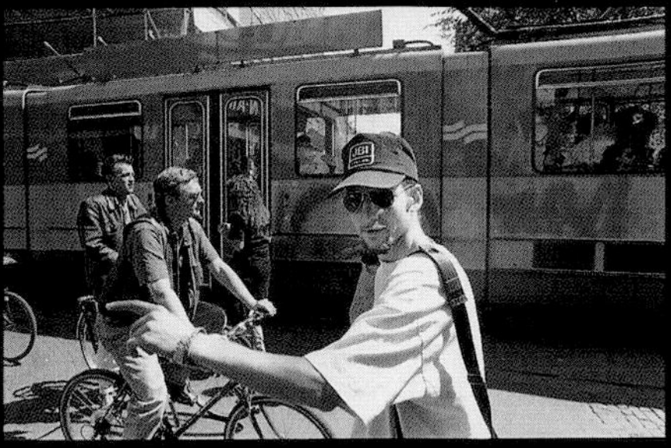
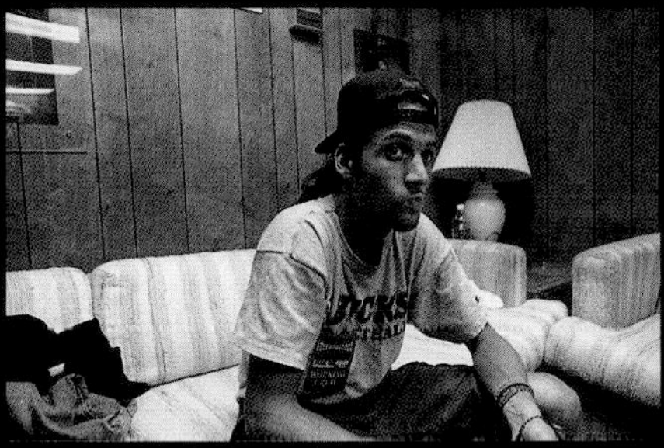
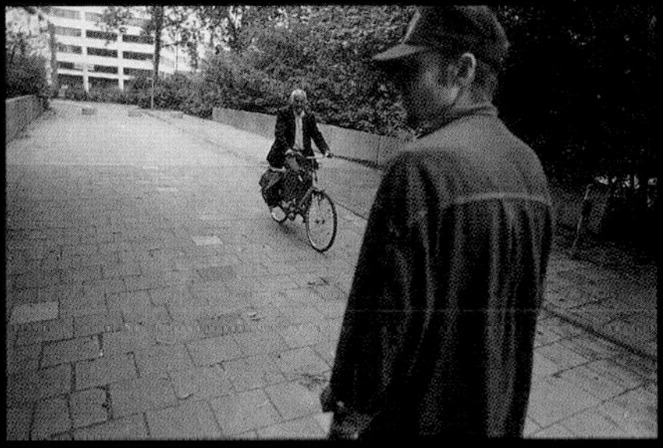
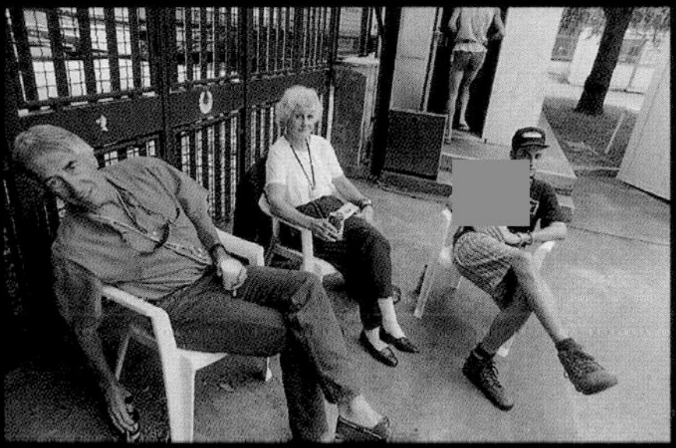
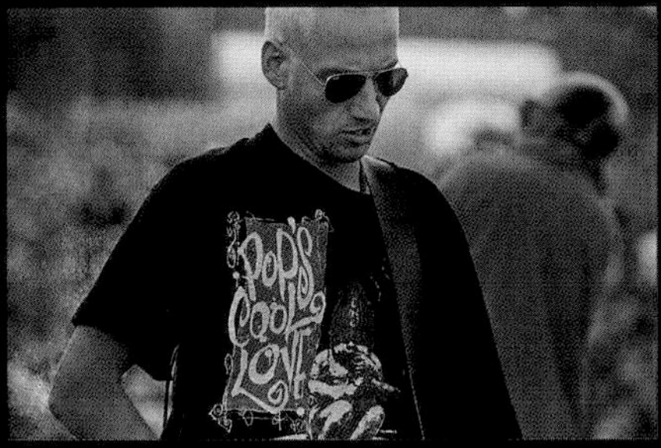
POPS
COOL
LOVE
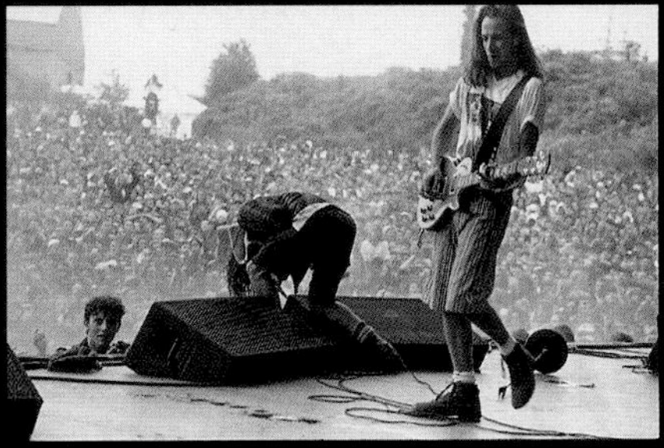
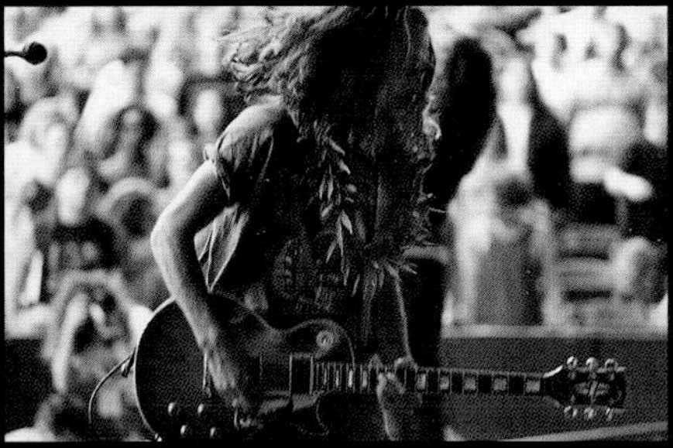
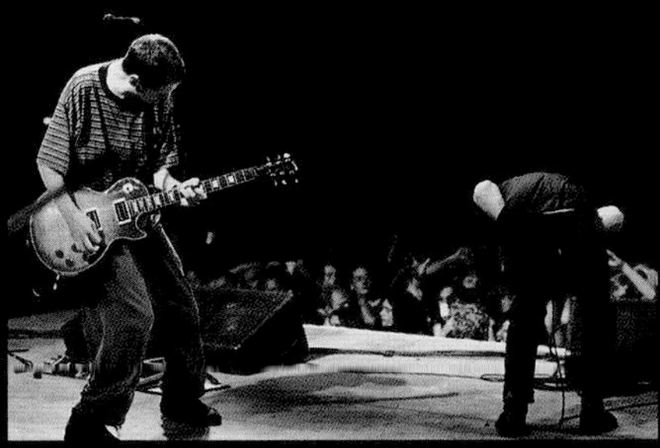
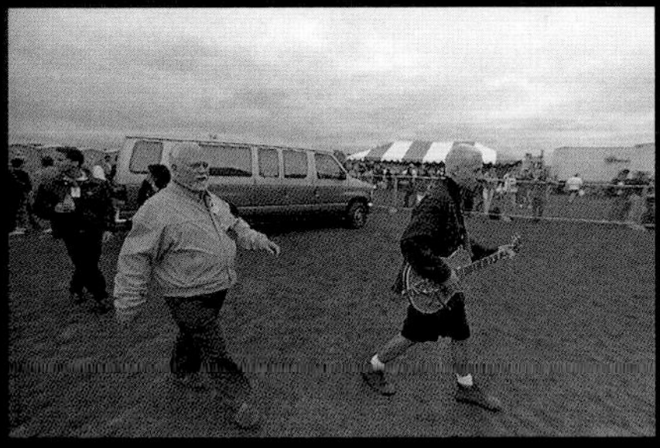
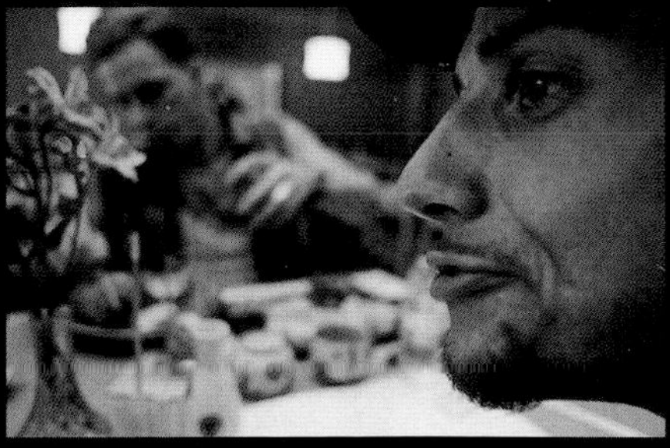

PEARL JAMN IT

I always noticed, and finally confronted Eddie with, something that he is master of, and something that I, as a performer, have never seemed to manage. And it's something that has bothered me immensely: it is economy of movement. Eddie has struck me, watching him for years, as one of the most charismatic but almost stock-still performers I've seen, at least since Lou Reed in 1977. He knows, instinctively I think, the exact moment of a song when a single hand gesture, a wave, a shift from one foot to the other, or an aquiline glance into the middle distance will create a rippled shudder through a room or across a crowd. No one, short of Bob Dylan or Lou Reed, in my vast experience, has such absolute control and charisma in being completely STILL. It annoys me and I am very jealous of it. So there, Eddie Vedder, you bastard. Great chunks of repeating and overlapping guitar, a meandering-until-it-nails-you-in-the-forehead melody, and a small wave of the hand. Colossal.

with love,
Michael Stipe

Michael Stipe

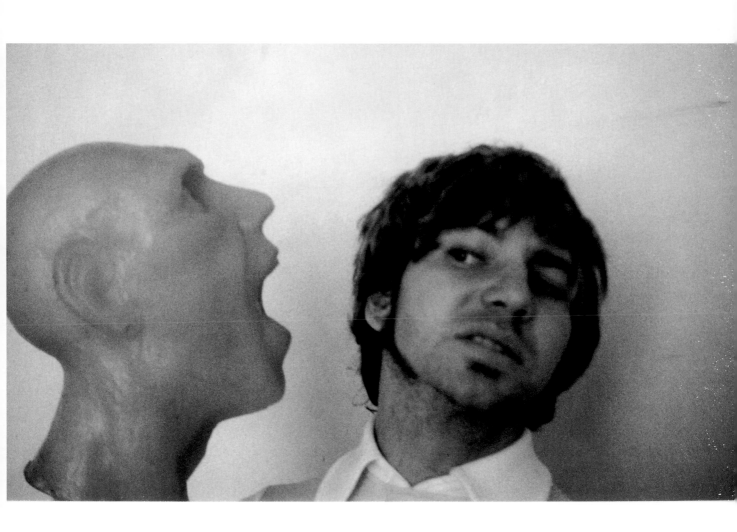

Since the early '90s, I had always had a feeling that somehow Ed and I would end up friends. We had some mutual friends and I guess I could feel his love of the ocean coming through some lyrics. We eventually met at some weird Grammy party in LA but got to know each other a little better in OZ when Pearl Jam was touring the Gold Coast and he came for a surf with a few of us. That night we went to the concert and he invited Rob Machado on stage with them for the encore. I was a little nervous and then the lights came on. I swore if Rob went up that I would, but he never showed and I got scared and went back to my seat, a choice I may always regret.

My best surf memories of ours are probably when we got him up on a short board for the first time and when we took him out to Waimea Bay on the North Shore of Hawaii. I'm not sure if Eddie was totally trusting me when I told him he wouldn't get his hair wet if he didn't want to, but it held true. The day before was about 30- to 40-foot faces, big enough to run the Eddie Aikau Invitational. The swell had backed off to about half the size the next day but still with some waves of up to 25-foot faces. There were only a few people out and Eddie stayed in the deep water channel building up his confidence and observing for most of the surf, just checking it out until he was "Ready Eddie." He must have had that saying running through his head, "Eddie Would Go!" after the great water man, Eddie Aikau, who was ironically lost at sea when his boat, *Hokulei'a,* capsized off the south coast of Hawaii en route to Tahiti. Eddie had shown up the day before to catch the day's action but now he wanted some of his own. I guess an hour of watching was enough. I helped him line up and a set approached. I yelled at him to go and he just paddled for his life, or the loss of it. He was perfectly positioned on the corner of the peak and started flying down the face, jumping to his feet just in time. The wave exploded and Eddie raced to the channel, outrunning the beast. That's how I remember it. Quite impressive for a first-time session at a wave many thought was impossible to survive, let alone ride, before it was ever done. I can't say he tamed the beast at Teahupo'o in Tahiti, but he was also there to witness some of the most incredible surf I have ever seen, saying in a letter to me after that it was like "watching an earthquake from the middle of a hurricane." After the surf at Waimea, Eddie looked me in the eyes and said it was the most intense thing he had ever done in his life. Having heard stories of 40-foot stage dives from other people, I was feeling pretty proud to have shared that experience with him.

A quick note about E.V. . . . He's not always available, but when he is, he is totally available. Sometimes you think you'll never hear from him again, but when you do, he really connects and it's something you remember for a long time. He is a good friend to many people.

Sincerely,
Kelly Slater

Kelly Slater

So here's how my Lance story starts, and let me first say
that since meeting Lance "officially" through Pearl Jam he has become one of my
dearest friends, and I have become a lucky collector of much of his work, including
my own wedding photos.

I grew up in Seattle, so for years at different punk rock shows or skate spots around
the city I would see this smiling, red-headed guy in a leather jacket. It was almost as
if we knew each other, but didn't. I'm sure we nodded to each other in recognition
hundreds of times. I knew him as "that photographer dude."

It was only after he came on one of the early Pearl Jam tours as the tour photographer that I got to know him. We hit it off instantly. Firstly, we can both waste
incredible amounts of time talking to anyone about anything. The two of us were a
match made in heaven. Most importantly though, where the band was concerned,
he just sort of seemed to "get it." As a tour manager, I didn't have to treat him
as some "special" photographer, rather, just one of the guys. Which, incidentally,
Lance loves being.

When it came to his photos, you could hardly ever tell if he was really working. I
only mean this in the most complimentary way possible. It never seemed as if he
was fighting for space for the perfect photo; instead, he just became part of the
landscape and let you see how it happened when people weren't being self-
conscious of a camera staring at them. He has the same ability when it comes
to photographing the band and life around them when they aren't onstage. I have
specific memories of good times in hotel lobbies or parties where I had no idea
Lance was even taking pictures, and am often amazed to see photos from those
very moments that capture the way we were actually feeling.

When I say that in regard to Pearl Jam, Lance just sort of seemed to "get it," I'm
sure that a good number of you out there must know what I mean. Pearl Jam
could never really be described as an "easy" band to work with. They are an unusual group of five pretty different personalities, all artists, and one manager, who
have done their best to eschew traditional publicity and do things their own way.
The hardest part of working for a band like Pearl Jam is figuring out what they want,
when they may not be sure themselves. It is a rather fine line to walk, but as an
artist, Lance always seems to transcend that. I won't say he has always done so
without his share of headaches, but as with anything worth doing, there is usually
some difficulty.

The fact that Lance is still there working with Pearl Jam only serves to make his art
more pure. He has a phenomenal understanding and friendship with this band. To
see these images as they are seen through Lance's eyes is to see and understand
them as they happened.

—Eric Johnson

Eric Johnson

Since we're all communal creatures, the distance between who we are inside and who we become in order to fit in can be great and even painful. I don't know if this distance is greater for people in the worlds of show business and rock music than in other work, but given the emphasis on externals and approval, it may be. I say this as a preface to meeting Pearl Jam because the first thing that struck me is how its members are just the opposite. From the clothes they wear, which have the same thrift shop look onstage as off, to the music they create and play, which makes even a huge audience feel they are friends who just happened to drop by the Seattle basement where these musicians are playing their hearts out, they seem as devoted to shortening the distance between public image and private self as any poet or mystic.

The same is true of their valiant effort to defeat the gouging prices of Ticketmaster, to keep a night of music within the reach of ordinary people. It's also a reason why they've always pledged to make time for their own children and families and private lives. It's even true of their political activism.

I think I was at their first political press conference. We were in a black hole of a Washington, D.C., nightclub in the daytime, where Eddie Vedder spoke movingly about reproductive freedom—the right to decide for ourselves, without government interference, when and whether to have children—before that night's benefit concert for Voters for Choice, a bi-partisan political action committee that I had helped to start. He chose his words with thoughtfulness, and cited facts and life stories with care. I later learned that his feeling for this fundamental human right had come from his own experience as an adopted child.

Recently, I witnessed Mike McCready's efforts to help with the research, insurance, and legal problems of people dealing with chronic diseases. He himself has experienced Crohn's disease and so empathizes with how much more difficult this and other such lifelong conditions are for people with fewer resources. Like Eddie, he doesn't see real life as separate from creativity, but as a chance to extend it.

For anyone tired of machine-made songs and public images tailored by focus groups, it's this authenticity that makes Pearl Jam unique. It helps each of us to find our own music.

—Gloria Steinem

Gloria Steinem

I hated Lance when I first saw him and his Bopo Boy buddies terrorizing my friends at punk rock shows in Seattle in the early '80s. Over the next year, I would see him on the Ave in his leather jacket rolling on his skateboard and I could tell there was something different about him. Compared to his black-haired cohorts, he was approachable and friendly. After a few conversations, we dubbed the red-Afroed Lance "the Nice Bopo." I saw him at every punk rock event in the Northwest that decade.

He got his shit together, went to school, learned how to take a picture, and in the process, shot all of his friends for free, which included Mother Love Bone, the band I was in at the time. Like us, he was a work in progress when it came to his art; I found out that he was open to any crazy ideas we had about the next photo shoot.

When Pearl Jam got started, Lance was right there. He took all the early live shots of us. When the record company wanted some posed shots, we agreed that we needed to break away from the standard railroad track rock shots and create something more natural and candid. We took location scouting trips all over the city; my favorite trip to the Olympic Peninsula created the Vs. artwork. I started taking more pictures around that time, which I think pissed Lance off, and so he threatened to start "playing bass." I told him that he should and he helped form the killer Seattle power punk group, The Briefs.

Lance Romance has always been about the music and that's why it all works. He worked his ass off, took a lot of shit, bugged the hell out of us, and captured the band like nobody has since. Thanks for the memories, Lance.

—Jeff Ament

Jeff Ament

All I can say is the physical building that is Madison Square Garden was shaking and swaying from the floor to the rafters. Ask anyone who was there that night, they'll tell you. It was one of those moments that changes your perception, changes the way things feel and taste. The show was so high energy, afterwards I went back to my hotel and slept for two days straight.

—Ben Harper

Ben Harper

Meeting my friend Lance Mercer

It started like any other day at *SPIN* magazine, which is to say that there were more than a few of us with hangovers from staying up too late with whatever band or musician was in town. There was also the pervasive sense that, although we knew we had a magazine to put together, at any moment the whole thing might fall apart. It was all very hectic, in a total "this is rock 'n' roll" kind of way. But there was one person who brought calm to the house and who we trusted implicitly with our day-to-day survival—Suzy, our British receptionist. She greeted us at the door every morning (or early afternoon), screened our calls, and made sure that the food deliverymen were connected with their rightful hungry recipients. Suzy held us all together.

That is why it was more than a little shocking when, as happened one day in mid-1991, Suzy F@#CK%D up. But, as luck would have it, from what might have been a disastrous situation came great fortune for me: I was introduced to someone who would become not only a good friend, but a person whose art I respect and enjoy, and whose outlook on the world makes me happy every time I talk to him—someone who, through his photos, shares with the world an energy that's vibrant and alive. That person is Lance Mercer.

I'd just returned from one of my more enjoyable assignments spent interviewing the band Pearl Jam, whose music I'd fallen in love with and whose major-label debut, *Ten,* was scheduled for release within the year. Lance had sent *SPIN*'s art department his slides of the band to be considered as accompaniment for my piece. These were Lance's original slides existing nowhere else in the world. However, once they landed on *SPIN*'s doorstep, Suzy, executing a rare fumble, saw the package sitting at reception and handed it off to a messenger, who rode this parcel around on his bicycle, threw it on a pile in a corner of the messenger center's HQ, and promptly forgot about it.

That day—the one that started like any other—Suzy beeped me with a call from Lance. I picked up the phone and on the other end was an incredibly calm—considering the circumstances—guy who had for weeks been trying to find out just what had happened to the multitudes of original slides of Pearl Jam that he'd sent to the magazine. These one-of-a-kind, can't-be-replaced-or-duplicated photos meant much more than Lance's livelihood— they were amazing pictures of his friends. I hadn't been privy to the situation until that very minute, and Suzy didn't remember that she'd seen the slides, had touched them, and then sent them into oblivion. Sometimes even overachievers like Suzy have memory misfires.

So that day the search, along with my friendship with Lance, began in earnest. Slowly we unraveled the mystery that was the Pearl Jam slide no-show. There were hours spent cajoling Suzy into re-checking her delivery logbook, the slow recollection of the fact that the slides had actually been in and then sent out of her hands, the "Sorry, dude, that messenger doesn't work here anymore" drama, and finally the eureka moment when the package of slides was located on a lonely pile at the messenger's HQ. All throughout these excruciating steps, Lance remained gracious and totally Zen-like. I remember thinking, "This guy is so NOT a neurotic New Yorker," along with "I should be more like that," and finally, "I need to be this guy's friend." All that went through my mind until one day, months later, I got a chance to meet Lance and, no lie, my world has been a better place ever since.

Even though he lives on the other side of the country, the times Lance and I have shared have been 100 percent enhanced by my ability to look at his photographs and see his force inside of them. Lance's photos express him so completely: his spirit, his creativity. I always think that photographers, like writers, are the silent partners in their creations, because they make their art happen out of the public's eye and then release it into the world for others to interpret. But where writers interact with a blank page or screen, photographers must respond to something that already lives on the other side of the lens. Some use props or poses. But Lance, it seems to me, trusts himself to capture life as it unfolds in front of him. That strikes me as the ultimate in trust—not only of self, but of subject. There's no doubt that Lance has had in Pearl Jam great humanity and material to work with, but it's more than that. His vision is uncluttered and trusting. The seamlessness by which he delivers a full experience and vision to the viewer leaves an indelible imprint that's timeless, yet in the moment.

I love that about Lance's photography . . . I feel as if I'm standing next to him when I look at his shots. I'm glad that I get the chance to stand in that place, both literally and figuratively. I could go on and on, but suffice it to say, Suzy, wherever you are, thanks for the fumble!

—Lauren Spencer

Lauren Spencer

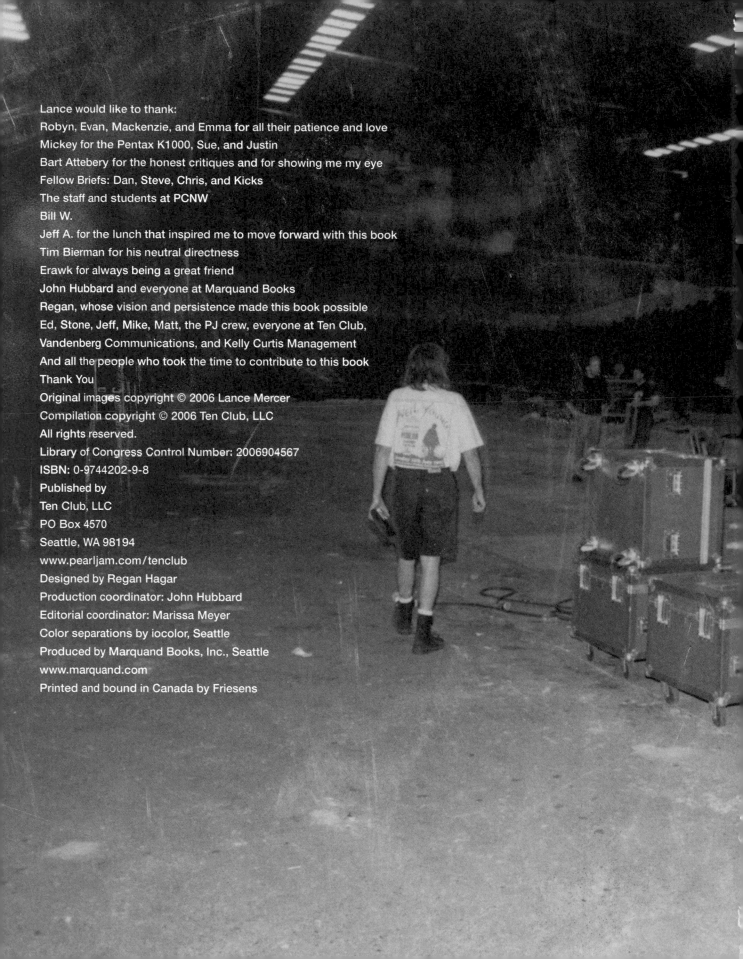

Lance would like to thank:
Robyn, Evan, Mackenzie, and Emma for all their patience and love
Mickey for the Pentax K1000, Sue, and Justin
Bart Attebery for the honest critiques and for showing me my eye
Fellow Briefs: Dan, Steve, Chris, and Kicks
The staff and students at PCNW
Bill W.
Jeff A. for the lunch that inspired me to move forward with this book
Tim Bierman for his neutral directness
Erawk for always being a great friend
John Hubbard and everyone at Marquand Books
Regan, whose vision and persistence made this book possible
Ed, Stone, Jeff, Mike, Matt, the PJ crew, everyone at Ten Club,
Vandenberg Communications, and Kelly Curtis Management
And all the people who took the time to contribute to this book
Thank You

Library of Congress Control Number: 2006904567
ISBN: 0-9744202-9-8
Published by
Ten Club, LLC
PO Box 4570
Seattle, WA 98194
www.pearljam.com/tenclub
Designed by Regan Hagar
Production coordinator: John Hubbard
Editorial coordinator: Marissa Meyer
Color separations by iocolor, Seattle
Produced by Marquand Books, Inc., Seattle
www.marquand.com
Printed and bound in Canada by Friesens